This is what happens

"An incisive reflection on how social forces constrain women's lives. ... Great for fans of Sylvia Plath, Doris Lessing's *The Golden Notebook*." Booklife

"I find the writing style very appealing ... An interesting mix of a memoir and a philosophical work, together with some amazing poetry. ... This is what happens ranks in my top five of books ever read." Mesca Elin, *Psychochromatic Redemption*

Thus Saith Eve

"Short, but definitely entertaining ... and serious between the lines." Lee Harmon, A Dubious Disciple Book Review

" ... a truly wonderful source of feminist fiction. In addition to being an extremely enjoyable and thought-provoking read, the monologues can also be used for audition and performance pieces." Katie M. Deaver, feminismandreligion.com

Snow White Gets Her Say

"Why isn't anyone doing this on stage? ... What a great night of theater that would be!" szferris, Librarything

"I loved the sassy voices in these stories, and the humor, even when making hard points." PJ O'Brien, Smashwords

Deare Sister

"You are clearly a writer of considerable talent, and your special ability to give expression to so many different characters, each in a uniquely appropriate style, makes your work fascinating and attractive. ... The pieces are often funny, sometimes sensitive, always

creative. But they contain an enormous load of anger, and that is where I have problems. ... I know at least one feminist who would read your manuscript with delight (unfortunately she is not a publisher), who would roar with laughter in her sharing of your anger. ..." rejection letter from Black Moss Press

Particivision and other stories

"... your writing is very accomplished. ... *Particivision and other stories* is authentic, well-written, and certainly publishable ..." rejection letter from Turnstone Press

"... engaging and clever ..." rejection letter from Lester & Orpen Dennys, Publishers

"As the title indicates, this collection of stories is about getting into the thick of things, taking sides, taking action, and speaking out loud and clear, however unpopular your opinion may be. ... refreshingly out of the ordinary." Joan McGrath, *Canadian Book Review Annual*

dreaming of kaleidoscopes

"... a top pick of poetry and is very much worth considering. ..." *Midwest Book Review*

Soliloquies: the lady doth indeed protest

"... not only dynamic, imaginative verse writing, but extremely intelligent and intuitive insight. ... I know many actresses who would love to get their hands on this material!" Joanne Zipay, Judith Shakespeare Company, NYC

"'Ophelia' is something of an oddity ... I found it curiously attractive." *Dinosaur*

UnMythed

"... A welcome relief from the usual male emphasis in this area. There is anger and truth here, not to mention courage." Eric Folsom, *Next Exit*

"... With considerable skill and much care, chris wind has extrapolated truths from mythical scenarios and reordered them in modern terms. ... Wind handles these myths with and intellect. Her voice suggests that the relationship between the consciousness of the myth-makers and modern consciousness is closer than we would think." Linda Manning, *Quarry*

"Personally, I would not publish this stuff. This is not to say it isn't publishable—it's almost flawless stylistically, perfect form and content, etc., etc. It's perverse: satirical, biting, caustic, funny. Also cruel, beyond bitter, single-minded with a terminally limited point of view, and this individual may have read Edith Hamilton's Mythology but she/he certainly doesn't perceive the essential meanings of these myths. Or maybe does and deliberately twists the meaning to suit the poem. Likewise, in the etymological sense. Editorial revisions suggested? None, it's perfect. Market potential/readership targets: Everyone—this is actually marketable—you could sell fill Harbourfront reading this probably. General comments: You could actually make money on this stuff." anonymous reader report for a press that rejected the ms

Satellites Out of Orbit

"*Satellites Out of Orbit* is an excellent and much recommended pick for unique fiction collections." Michael Dunford, *Midwest Book Review*

"... I also love the idea of telling the story from the woman's perspective, especially when the woman is only mentioned in passing in the official story, or not mentioned at all. ..." Shana, Tales of Minor Interest

"Our editorial board loved it. Our readers said it was the most feminist thing they've read in a long time." rejection letter from publisher

As I the Shards Examine / Not Such Stuff

"*Not Such Stuff* challenges us to rethink some of our responses to Shakespeare's plays and opens up new ways of experiencing them. ... " Jeff, secondat.blogspot.com

"This world premiere collection of monologs derive from eight female Shakespearian characters speaking from their hearts, describing aspects of their lives with a modern feminist sensibility. Deconstructing the traditional interpretations of some of the most fiercely fascinating female characters of all time, the playwright is able to "have at it" and the characters finally have their say. And oh, what tales they have to weave. ..." Debbie Jackson, dctheatrescene.com

Let Me Entertain You

"I found 'Let Me Entertain You' very powerful and visually theatrical." Ines Buchli

"I will never forget 'Let Me Entertain You.' It was brilliant." Kate Hurman

ProVocative

"Timely, thought-provoking, dark, and funny!" Kevin Holm-Hudson, WEFT

"… a great job making a point while being entertaining and interesting. … Overall this is a fine work, and worth listening to." Kevin Slick, *gajoob*

The Art of Juxtaposition

"A cross between poetry, performance art, and gripping, theatrical sound collages. … One of the most powerful pieces on the tape is 'Let Me Entertain You.' I sat stunned while listening to this composition." Myke Dyer, *Nerve*

"We found [this to be] unique, brilliant, and definitely not 'Canadian'. ... We were more than impressed with the material. *The Art of Juxtaposition* is filling one of the emptier spaces in the music world with creative and intelligent music-art." rejection letter from a record company

"Controversial feminist content. You will not be unmoved." Bret Hart, *Option*

"I've just had a disturbing experience: I listened to *The Art of Juxtaposition*. Now wait a minute; Canadian musicians are not supposed to be politically aware or delve into questions regarding sexual relationships, religion, and/or sex, racism, rape. They are supposed to write nice songs that people can tap their feet to and mindlessly inebriate themselves to. You expect me to play this on my show?" Travis B., CITR

"Wind mixes biting commentary, poignant insight and dark humor while unflinchingly tackling themes such as rape, marriage (as slavery), christianity, censorship, homosexuality, the state of native Americans, and other themes, leaving no doubt about her own strong convictions upon each of these subjects. Her technique is often one in which two or more sides to each theme are juxtaposed against one another (hence, the tape's title). This is much like her *Christmas Album* with a voice just as direct and pointed. Highly recommended." Bryan Baker *gajoob*

"Thanks for *The Art of Juxtaposition* ... it really is quite a gem! Last Xmas season, after we aired 'Ave Maria' a listener stopped driving his car and phoned us from a pay phone to inquire and express delight." John Aho, CJAM

"Liked *The Art of Juxtaposition* a lot, especially the feminist critiques of the bible. I had calls from listeners both times I played 'Ave Maria.'" Bill Hsu, WEFT

"Every time I play *The Art of Juxtaposition* (several times by this point), someone calls to ask about it/you." Mars Bell, WCSB

"The work is stimulating, well-constructed, and politically apt with regard to sexual politics. (I was particularly impressed by 'I am Eve.')" Andreas Brecht Ua'Siaghail, CKCU

"We have found *The Art of Juxtaposition* to be quite imaginative and effective. When I first played it, I did not have time to listen to it before I had to be on air. When I aired it, I was transfixed by the power of it. When I had to go on mike afterward, I found I could hardly speak! To say the least, I found your work quite a refreshing change from all the fluff of commercial musicians who whine about lost love etc. Your work is intuitive, sensitive, and significant!" Erika Schengili, CFRC

"Interesting stuff here! Actually this has very little music, but it has sound bits and spoken work. Self-declared 'collage pieces of social commentary'. …very thought-provoking and inspiring." *No Sanctuary*

more at
chriswind.net
and
chriswind.com

by chris wind

prose
This is what happens
Thus Saith Eve
Snow White Gets Her Say
Deare Sister
Particivision and other stories

poetry
dreaming of kaleidoscopes
Soliloquies: the lady doth indeed protest
UnMythed
Paintings and Sculptures

mixed genre
Satellites Out of Orbit
Excerpts

stageplays
As I the Shards Examine / Not Such Stuff
The Ladies' Auxiliary
Snow White Gets Her Say
The Dialogue
Amelia's Nocturne

performance pieces
I am Eve
Let Me Entertain You

audio work
ProVocative
The Art of Juxtaposition

Paintings

and

Sculptures

Paintings

and

Sculptures

chris wind

magenta

Published by Magenta

Paintings and Sculptures
© 1991, 2021 by chris wind
2nd Edition

ISBN 978-1-926891-15-6 paperback
ISBN 978-1-926891-19-4 epub
ISBN 978-1-926891-18-7 pdf

All rights reserved. Without limiting the rights under copyright reserved above, no part of this publication may be reproduced, stored in or introduced into a retrieval system, or transmitted, in any form, or by any means (electronic, mechanical, photocopying, recording, or otherwise) without the prior written permission of both the copyright owner and the above publisher of this book.

This is a work of fiction. Names, characters, places, brands, media, and incidents are either the product of the author's imagination or are used fictitiously. The author acknowledges the trademarked status and trademark owners of various products referenced in this work of fiction, which have been used without permission. The publication/use of these trademarks is not authorized, associated with, or sponsored by the trademark owners.

www.chriswind.net

Cover design by chris wind
Image credit Ingo Menhard / Alamy Stock Photo
Formatting and layout design by Elizabeth Beeton

Library and Archives Canada Cataloguing in Publication

Title: Paintings and sculptures / Chris Wind.
Names: wind, chris, author.
Description: Second edition. | Poems. | Previously published: Sundridge, Ontario: Chris Wind/Magenta, 1991.
Identifiers: Canadiana (print) 20200395092 | Canadiana (ebook) 20200395122 | ISBN 9781926891156 (softcover) | ISBN 9781926891187 (PDF) | ISBN 9781926891194 (EPUB)
Classification: LCC PS8595.I592 P34 2021 | DDC C811/.54—dc23

acknowledgements

"sparkling spring water" *Rampike* (1998) 9.2

"Trans-Canada Tailings" *Canadian Dimension* (December 1995) 29.6

"The Three Graces" *Next Exit* (Winter 1992) 20

"Put Your Foot Down" *Next Exit* (Winter 1992) 20

"Sunday Afternoon in Algonquin Park" *The New Quarterly* (Fall 1992)

"Playing Solitaire" *The New Quarterly* (Fall 1992)

"woman with broom" *Prism International* (January 1988) 20.2

"the thinker" *Canadian Woman Studies* (Winter 1998) 17.4; *Bogg* (Fall 1989) 61

Thanks to Lossie Murray-Pigeon for her excellent editorial advice.

Thanks to *The New Quarterly* and the people of Ontario (through the Ontario Arts Council) for their support.

Paintings

The Persistence of Memory	3
The Creation of Adam	4
Sunday Afternoon in Algonquin Park	5
The Last Supper	6
The Three Graces	7
Venus of San Francisco	8
American Gothic	9
Mona	10
Luncheon on the Grass	11
The Death of Socrates	12
Cupid	13
Still Life	14
Woman with Broom	15
The Nativity	16
No Tide™ in Turin	17
The Nuclear Family	18
Passing Time	19
Sparkling Spring Water	20
Put Your Foot Down	21
Mug Shots	24
I'm Growing Just As Fast As I Can	25
My Supervisor's Calendar	26
Dressed to Kill (Recruitment Poster No. 1)	27
There's No Life Like It! (Recruitment Poster No. 2)	28
We *Have* the Cure for Cancer.	29
Potlach	30

Balls

1st panel	33
2nd panel	34
3rd panel	35
4th panel	36
5th panel	37
6th panel	38
7th panel	39

Sculptures

David, after Goliath	43
Venus	44
The Statue of Liberty	45
Porch of the Maidens	46
Rape of the Sabine Woman	48
Nike, Goddess of Victory	49
The Thinker	50
Lady of Justice	51
Wheels: Status Symbols	52
The Perfect Pedestal	53
Peacekeeper	54
Domestic Dispute	55
War Monument	56
Trans-Canada Tailings	57
Just Desserts	58

Paintings

> sometimes in the morning
> on that bare dressing table
> in the corner of the bedroom
> i can see my heart
> hanging
> my ruby heart
> hanging over   over
>   the
>   edge
> bleeding onto the floor

The Persistence of Memory

God was giving him something
I'm sure of that
look at the way his hand is,
fingers folding around   nothing
it must've gotten painted over
so what was it
a Big Mac?   a Mars bar?
no, this is the creation of the first *man*
I know, a Molson Golden!
no, look at the extension —
it had to have been …
a gun?

The Creation of Adam

a forest full of emily carr trees
rich heartwood warm to the touch
so curving and alive you can hear them hum

each tree with an umbrella
i kid you not
right out of Seurat's 'Sunday Afternoon
  on the Island of la Grande Jatte'
seeming so rigid and erect
proper (sunscreen or raincoat?)
but a little surreal

and yet
as logical as a city squirrel
with a gas mask

Sunday Afternoon in Algonquin Park

this is more like it
a bunch of men are watching the game
there are twelve of them, cheering, yelling,
sprawled on the couch, the chairs, the floor
and one, front row center, in the lazyboy
(must be his house this rec room is in)
they all have a bottle of beer in one hand
and a chunk of pizza in the other

there's some serious emotion going on here
passionate talk
about what happened and why
what should be happening
and what's gonna happen
all accompanied with nudges and backslapping
(at the end they'll be hugging)
there are differences of opinion
heated exchanges
but their devotion to the game
is never in question

(except for the guy in the corner
the one with the glasses
who brought a book)
(he was going to bring a woman
for god's sake!)

The Last Supper

> neither Botticelli
>   nor Tintoretto
>   nor Raphael
> had this courage—
>
> to show three naked men
> singing and dancing,
> to say men could embody
> joy, charm, and beauty

The Three Graces

> it looks the same:
> opulent nude reclining
> on one of those sofas
>   look again
> she's smiling? she wasn't smiling before?
>   and?
>   look at her hand,
>   so lifelessly covering her crotch?
> oh! her finger!
> she's funning herself!

Venus of San Francisco

> Barbie and Ken
> side by side
> effervescent smiles
> unblinking eyes
> plastic flesh
> hollow hollow

American Gothic

she isn't smiling
she didn't feel like smiling
come on, he coaxed
just a little smile, for me? he pleaded
a young woman should never be without a smile, he chided
a face as beautiful as yours—he flattered
she gave up, she gave in
she smiled
it felt fake, it felt stupid
but i'm smiling, okay
are you happy now?
he scheduled another sitting

she still wasn't smiling
she didn't feel like smiling
come on, he coaxed again
just a little smile—
to thine own self be true
she refused
he felt threatened
it was a sacrilege
so he righted the wrong
tried to project the curve of her lips
didn't do so well
he scheduled another sitting

what's the big deal
she grinned
this smile could be the face
of any number of thoughts
it's a mystery only to minds
not expecting, unable to consider
anything on a woman but that
vapid shallow simple girlish
smile

he went back to the original
unsmiling

Mona

it's not working
this reversal—
i have undressed the men
and clothed the woman,
and i've left them at the lakeside,
but now she looks like a prude
instead of a prostitute,
just as vulnerable,
just as subordinate,
equally an object
of their scorn or indifference.

maybe it's in the numbers—
but what do i do
with a naked man
in the presence of
two fully-clothed women?

(if i told you they were artists
and he was their model,
would you believe me?)

Luncheon on the Grass

they rejected the sentence that he proposed—
the reward of a distinguished citizen:
honourable maintenance at public expense
(he figured he was at least as valuable
as the jock who won the chariot race
at the Olympics)
—and decided again, on death

so he sits, the same, in that stone cell
reaching for the hemlock,
   still speaking out,
      arm upraised—
surrounded not by that group of hysterical men
weeping and wailing, flailing about

but by everyone ever charged
with neglecting the gods of the state—
  Pope Joan and Joan of Arc
  Galileo and Darwin
  Thoreau and Russell and all the men
    who would not be soldiers
  Katya Komisaruk and the Greenham women
  the Temagami defenders and various Greenpeacers
or corrupting the morals of the young—
  Goody Glover, Oscar Wilde
  Rosa Parks, Margaret Sanger
  Nikki Craft, Morgentaler

even as a mural, covering all four walls
there is not enough room
for those who question, examine, expose
for the good of the people who arrest them,
      imprison them,
   kill them—

no wonder, this time,
it's his *middle* finger
that's jabbing the air

The Death of Socrates

a little less chubby, yes
and a good fifteen, twenty years older
but there's something else—
i can't quite—
the heart's still there, amazingly
and the arrow, or some other weapon
that's it—

the grin.
he looks like my husband
  beating down the door of the shelter
or the guy who raped me last spring

Cupid

> this one's pretty standard
> there's a person, sitting
> in an upholstered chair
> feet up, reading the newspaper
> (light cast from a lamp in the corner)
> and another person
> different shape
> slightly different angle
> watching tv
> in their
> *living* room

Still Life

> in time, the rock of Sisyphus eroded ...
> now slowly she walks
> all along that barren beach
>   sweeping the sand back into the water

Woman with Broom

there is the stable
of rotting slivered beams
part of it has fallen apart
the rest is on a tilt

it's been raining
the dirt's mud,
where there's not much straw

the cows and pigs are standing about
it's daylight and you can see manure
everywhere

and there, half lying, half squatting
over where there's most straw
Mary
her legs are parted
straining wide
you can see the bruises
from riding all that way
nine months pregnant
and you can see the wet
dark red and thick
and the torn vulva and ripping flesh
and all the blood smeared on the inside of her thighs
and the membranous mucous stuff partially gushed
onto the dirt
and on her face,
nothing but pain

The Nativity

> she's standing there
> holding up a sheet or something
> so gray it looks like a shroud
> and you can still see the smudges
> of a man's face on it
>
> she's crying,
> no, weeping is more like it
> her face is contorted,
> she's completely undone

No Tide™ in Turin

> this is another one of those 20th century things
> there is nothing on the canvas
> it's totally empty, totally white
> not even a black speck
> there is nothing, totally nothing
> i suspect it's called 'Study in White, No.3'

The Nuclear Family

in the center fore
a woman is sitting at a kitchen table
playing cards

it is an ordinary woman
fiftyish with brown hair
at an ordinary kitchen table
turquoise flecked arborite with shiny chrome legs
and you can tell by the cards
two ace piles underway and one king with a five-card genealogy
that it's an ordinary game

in the background
where the fridge and the cupboards might be
is a mural collage
newspaper clippings about Burger King and labour in Mexico
letters to the editor about bicycle lanes and certain pharmaceuticals
requests from Amnesty International, Energy Probe, Civil Liberties
articles exposing Fabergé, Kimberly-Clark, Ontario Hydro, General Electric
pamphlets detailing the drug trade on playgrounds and black-bashing
factsheets on styrofoam and pesticides and nuclear accidents

nevertheless she sits there
'just minding her own business'
playing cards

Passing Time

a water cooler
plain, ordinary
the kind you see
everywhere

but drawn inside throughout the water
is a bunch of those

    twinkling   atomic
        energy
                      spirographs
and
        radioactive
pinwheels

(it gives new meaning to)
Sparkling Spring Water

little girl	ballerina	oriental woman	foxy lady
tiny feet		dwarfed feet	size fives
	be-ribboned	bound	strapped into
on tippy toe	en pointe		four-inch stilettos

Put Your Foot Down

the next painting isn't really a painting at all
it's a photograph
actually, it's lots of photographs
arranged in pairs
in black and white

i look closely at the first pair:
on the left, a seedy-looking character
*convicted of theft under
and assault with a deadly weapon;*
on the right, an ordinary-looking man
in his best suit and tie
Mr. Arnold, the victim's father

the next pair is somewhat similar:
a kind of ragged-looking man, unshaven
convicted of break and enter on the left;
the man on the right could be my uncle
Mr. Jansen, homeowner, who says
'Thank goodness for the Neighbourhood Watch program!'

i continue scanning the pairs
thinking what's the point
when my eye is caught by a mistake—
the little photos have gotten mixed up—
a man stressed out and a little sloppy
is on the right, identified as
*the father of a six-year-old boy
who developed cataracts after
treatment with MER/29;*
the man on the left wears a lab coat
and is *Dr. Evert Van Maanen,
Director of Biological Sciences at
William S. Merrel Toxicology Lab,
charged with knowingly making
false, fictitious, and fraudulent statements
to the FDA about MER/29*
no—the photos are right—

i go on to the next pair:
on the right, someone whose name
i can't recall, one of thousands,
a victim of Minimata disease;
and on the left, in a three-piece suit, *E. Nishida
found guilty of involuntary manslaughter
in the death of six people
who ate fish contaminated
by his plant's mercury waste*

i skip over the next few,
then stop at the last pair:
an older, haggard-looking man on the right
is *William Whitlock, a retired civil engineer*
exposed to dangerous levels of radiation;
and on the left,
looking very competent in his technician's coat
James Floyd, former Supervisor of Operations
at Three Mile Island, convicted of cheating
on the Nuclear Regulatory Commission Operating exams

Mug Shots

filling the entire hallway
and then some,
down one side and up the other,
one hundred small pencil drawings
neatly hung in a long, long row

the first, year one, a seed,
further along, a little sprout,
then a bona fide sapling
that becomes, barely,
throughout the years,
this small, thin thing,
at year twenty-two, a little taller
year thirty-eight, a little thicker
but so slowly i swear
years fifty-four through seventy-nine
are the same drawing

eventually i stand at one hundred years
in front of a tree
four inches in diameter

I'm Growing Just As Fast As I Can

> Miss February
> wears only skis and boots
> it's a shot from behind
> she's bending over
> legs spread to snowplow

My Supervisor's Calendar
(I don't think I'll get that promotion)

> three young men and one young woman
> uniform in military dress
> clean, shiny, and freshly pressed
> plastered on the streetcorner wall
> tall and proud
> with eyes bright as buttons
> and waitress smiles

Dressed to Kill
(Recruitment Poster No. 1)

a sorry bunch:
one stump of a man is in a wheelchair
wrists strapped down
so his arms don't fall off
torso strapped in
so he doesn't topple

on his left stands a figure
from a horror show
eyes unfocussed in sunken sockets
a foot long incision
stitched up his skull
we're not quite sure
he'll be able
to brush his teeth by himself

and on the right, a man
holds his bladder in his hands

the other two feature assorted injuries:
mangled parts, missing parts,
perhaps replacement parts
but both are morphined out of their minds
so for now it doesn't matter

There's No Life Like It!
(Recruitment Poster No. 2)

> 1. Cease the production of all ozone-destroying chemicals.
>
> 2. Illegalize the nuclear industry.
>
> 3. Ban the use of all carcinogens in all industries, especially but not exclusively, the agricultural industry and all manufacturing industries.

We *Have* the Cure for Cancer.

Earth's Budget	
armaments, weapons	$973.4 billion
education	701.2 billion
health	590.5 billion
international peace-keeping	.3 billion

Potlach*

* "Potlach is not only a gift. In its most impressive form, potlach consists in the solemn destruction of wealth. A tribal chief presents himself before his rival and has a number of slaves slaughtered before his rival's eyes. The rival must retaliate by slaughtering an even greater number of slaves. Potlach, then, is an act of ostentatious destruction, the aim of which is to intimidate the rival… and prove his own superiority." Franco Fornari

Balls

This is a series of sculptures,
each mounted on a panel
that is hung like a painting.

> two marbles
> one a steely, the other coloured
> dangle
> in a sandwich bag scrotum

The game of marbles is perhaps the first instance in a man's life of organized group behaviour focussing on balls. Sometimes the boy has a special bag for carrying his marbles. He does so quite proudly, often bragging to others about the quantity in his possession.

1st panel

> two golfballs
> pockmarked moons
> swing
> in a leather glove

This method of playing with balls is considered far more important than marbles. Men will give money to belong to clubs that will allow them to do it this way.

They do not give money to organizations that recycle waste or research contraception.

2nd panel

> two tennis balls
> green and fuzzy
> bulge
> in a pocket of racquet webbing

A man who plays with these balls can make over $250,000 per year.

A man who saves other people's lives makes less than half that.

And almost everyone else makes one-tenth of that.

3rd panel

> two shotputs
> solid, heavy
> sag
> in a pouch of knotted thong

Playing with these balls is an endeavour recognized by the Olympic Committee: this means that after years of serious daily practice, men will get together, every four years, to see who can throw one the farthest. A gold medal is given to that man.

An inner city teacher was raped by four of her students, and she is still teaching. She has not been given a gold medal.

4th panel

> two baseballs
> fingerprinted grey
> suspended
> in macraméd twine

Recently the government decided to spend 200 million dollars to build a place with a special roof so men could play with these balls and people could watch without getting wet or putting it off for another day.

The government decided not to spend that 200 million on homes for kids whose parents don't want them anymore or apartments for seniors on fixed incomes.

5th panel

> two soccer balls
> dirt-stained and scuffed
> drooped
> enclosed in mesh

At a recent soccer game, a fight broke out among the fans (these are people who find it exciting to watch other men play with balls), and three people were killed.

A similar battle over income tax reform or equal-pay-for-work-of-equal-value has never been reported.

6th panel

> two basketballs
> pebbly orange
> swell
> in a sack of netting

Several times a day, scores of these and other ball games are announced over radio networks, and major newspapers set aside an entire section for such news.

A separate section is not set aside for details about our path toward or from nuclear devastation or climate change.

7th panel

> # Sculptures

standing there, remembering,
just as Michelangelo saw him—

       sure and strong
    with pride, power
and an erection

David, after Goliath

        that classic female figure
          a universal standard—
            half   naked
draped
     in
         diaphanous
   white
                 arms chopped off
                    at the tricep
      immobilized in stone
    —displayed in a cage,
                  labelled
     "go-go girl"

Venus

strong, free
and at last
no joke;
a man stands proudly
holding the torch

The Statue of Liberty

a book is balanced
upon each one's
head
a wet t-shirt
curves
in
fixed
folds
they stand still
in tight jeans
one
knee
bent
they are sweet sixteen
four of them
poised
along the ledge
of a verandah
in north toronto

a book is balanced
upon each one's
head
a wet t-shirt
curves
in
fixed
folds
they stand still
in tight jeans
one
knee
bent
they are sweet sixteen
four of them
poised
along the ledge
of a verandah
in north toronto

Porch of

a book is balanced
  upon each one's
    head
  a wet t-shirt
    curves
in
fixed
  folds
  they stand still
    in tight jeans
        one
            knee
      bent
they are sweet sixteen
  four of them
    poised
  along the ledge
  of a verandah
  in north toronto

the Maidens

trained to be fast,
he has easily outrun her—
taller, heavier,
he lifts her off the ground—
using the strength of his work-muscled arm
he pins her pelvis against his chest—
his other arm reaches across her shoulders
and stops her from arching away—

her right arm flails for leverage
while her left pulls back, ready,
her fingers gripping tightly
                              the knife
that will even out the odds

Rape of the Sabine Woman

she is no longer fastening her sandal
it is fastened, has been for quite some time
and she is running
> she did not drop dead at the first marathon

she has run so far and so fast
all those voluminous draperies have been blown away
> besides, it wasn't a wet t-shirt contest

in mid-stride her muscled body
is more glorious
the drops of sweat on her skin
are like diamonds on ebony

and those wings—
huge and powerful, they certainly
put Mercury's little anklets to shame
but no,
she has, simply, arms
pumped and powerful
> a woman doesn't have to be supernatural to win

(oh—and the head—
she has one.)

Nike, Goddess of Victory

strong, solid
         chin on hand
    right elbow on thigh
left arm across knee
                leaning forward
    breasts filling in the spaces
            between the lines

The Thinker

she looks like a street vendor in summer
no, an optician's sidewalk salesperson;
she stands beside a placard display
all sizes and shapes in current styles,
a Buddy Holly pair from the fifties,
and a rhinestone-studded cat-eye pair,
further down, some granny glasses
even a kid's Mickey Mouse pair in red;
and, to be truthful,
there's some sunglasses, over-priced,
as well as a pair that's rose-coloured;
on the little table, in front,
a magnifying glass and a microscope

she stands beside:
nonchalantly polishing her own glasses
with what looks like a blindfold

Lady of Justice

two figurines
simply juxtaposed:

person pulling   person pushing
a rickshaw   a wheelchair

Wheels: Status Symbols

      fixed upon a pedestal
  that position of privilege and prestige
          is a throne of sorts
                    worn by the weight
                of so many women
   with manacles for ankle and wrist

The Perfect Pedestal

this one's a parade float
coming after, perhaps, the Boy Scouts
and before the Knights of Columbus
it's a flatbed trailer
fifty or sixty feet long, maybe ten feet wide
decorated with crepe paper in patriotic colours
and raised upon it
in the great tradition of display
and public celebration of our achievements
  an MX missile

two hundred times as destructive
as the Little Boy dropped on Hiroshima
so covering the four sides of the base, photos
of 13 million buildings in rubble
28 million people, cancerous or deformed
15 million people, burned, blasted, catatonic with shock
and bodies, 14 million, charred

Peacekeeper

he's wearing steel-toed construction boots
you can see the green triangle
and jeans and a t-shirt;
he could be dancing, arms up,
torso leaning, leg flung forward—
but that steel-toed construction boot
is about to make contact
with her face
bruised, puffy, and eight inches from the floor
not quite steady on her sagging shoulders
her crumpling body
the kick will certainly smash her jaw
if it doesn't snap her neck

Domestic Dispute

the quintessential soldier
very male
very eighteen
showing in his stance
he's proud to kill
and unaffected by pain

he's wearing a helmet
baggy multipocketed pants and jacket
thick-soled army boots
backpack, gas mask, canteen
and a gun—

but instead of the Rambo
ribbon of bullets
slung diagonal across his chest
there's a Miss America banner

    "GO

        LEMMINGS

            GO!"

War Monument

in the next room
someone has sculpted Canada
into a huge relief map:
as i walk the length of the room
i notice the teeny-weeny lobster traps,
the CN Tower of course, and the Skydome,
the patchwork prairies, Lake Louise,
the chairlifts at Whistler;
it's large, no doubt about it,
with lots of detail,
and it'd be of no consequence
except that
all along the highway
                from coast to coast
winding its way
       throughout
   the land
this stuff is piled—
higher than the dinky cars
placed at the intersections—
garbage, i guess

but it's glowing

(from one tiny
maple-leaf signpost
to the next)

Trans-Canada Tailings

the slice of apple pie looks fine
so does the cherry tart
except they're surrounded by
little spice bottles
(oil and flour finger smeared)
labelled Lindane, Amaranth, Dimethoate,
Fenpropathrin, Heptenophos, Mevinphos,
Parathion, Alpha HCH, DDT—
each marked with that
little skull-and-bones

Just Desserts